You may talk of your harp, your piano or lute
But nothing could sound like the ould Orange flute.

A traditional comic ballad about a flute with a mind of its own and a very particular taste in music. . .

Hector McDonnell, son of the 13th Earl of Antrim, was born in 1947. His educational career took him from Eton to Munich, Oxford, and to Vienna, where he studied sculpture under the leading Austrian sculptor Wotruba. His work has been exhibited in galleries in London, Belfast, Dublin, Paris, Brussels, Munich, Vienna and Stuttgart. In 1979 he won an important German art competition, the Darmstädter Kunstpreis, and as a result of this had a major retrospective exhibition in the Matildenhöhe in Darmstadt the following year.

In 1982, he illustrated *Saturday Night in York Street*, a collection of poems by Belfast dock-worker, John Campbell, and his etchings illustrating *The Ballad of William Bloat*, a poem by Raymond Calvert, were also published that year.

Although no fluter himself, he was recently elected Honorary President of the Belfast Folk Festival.

He divides his time between his home in London, and the family seat at Glenarm, County Antrim.

The Ould Orange Flute

The Ould Orange Flute

illustrated by Hector McDonnell

The Blackstaff Press

to
Colquito, Hannah
and Lalla,
with
all my love

In the
County
Tyrone,
near the
town
of
Dungannon,
where
many's the
ruction
myself
had a han' in,

Bob Williamson
lived,
a weaver
by trade,
and
all of us
thought him
a
stout
Orange blade.

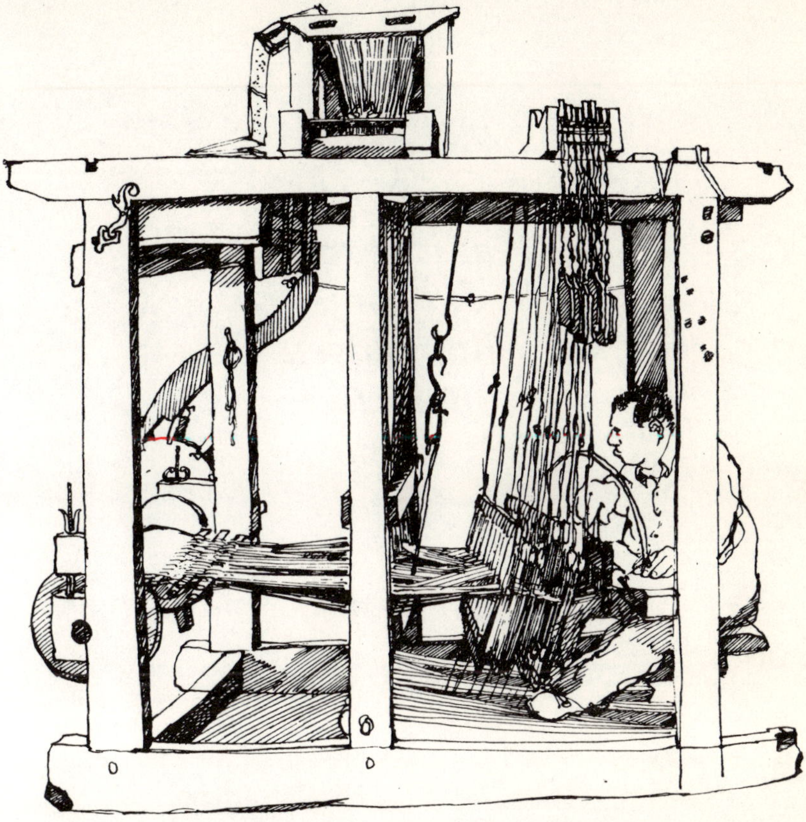

On the
Twelfth of July,
as it yearly
did come,
Bob played
on the flute
to the
sound
of
the drum.

WE WILL NOT HAVE HOME RULE

You may talk
of your harp,
your piano
or lute,
but nothing
could sound
like
the ould
Orange
flute.

NO
SURRENDER

But Bob
the deceyver,
he took us all
in,
for he married
a Papish
called
Bridget McGinn,

Turned Papish
himself,
and forsook
the ould cause
that gave us
our freedom,
religion,
and laws.

ACT OF UN

Now,
the boys
in the townland
made comment
upon it,
and Bob
had to fly
to the
province
of Connaught.

He flew
with his wife,
and his fixin's
to boot,
and along
with the others
the ould
Orange
flute.

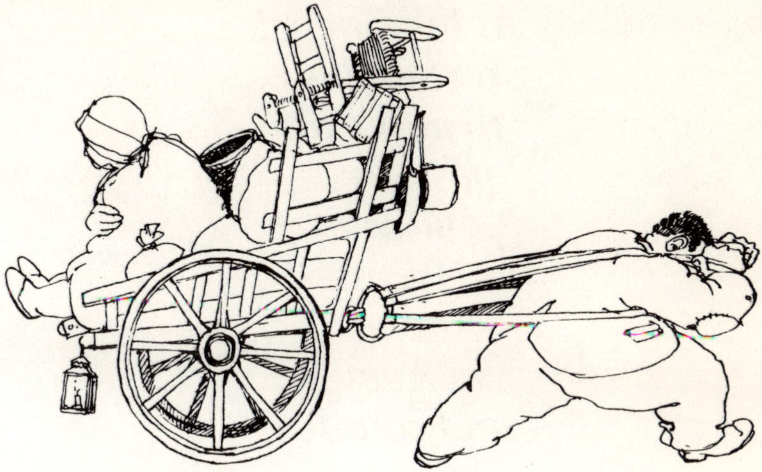

At the Chapel
on Sundays
to atone for
past deeds,
he said
'Paters'
and
'Aves'
and counted
his beads,

Till,
after some time,
at the priest's
own desire,
he went
with his ould flute
to play
in the
choir.

He went
with his ould flute
to play
in the Mass,
but
the instrument
shivered
and
sighed,
Oh alas!

When
he blew it
and fingered
and made
a great noise,
the flute
would play only
'The Protestant
Boys'.

Bob jumped
and he started
and got
in a splutter,
and threw
the ould flute
in the
Bless'd
Holy Water;
he thought
that this charm
might bring
some other sound.

When he blew it
again,
it played
'Croppies Lie Down',
and all
he could whistle
and finger
and blow,
to play
Papish music
he found it
no go.

'Kick the Pope',
'The Boyne Water'
and such like
it would sound,
but one
Papish squeak
in it
couldn't be
found.

At a
council
of priests
that was held
the next day,
they decided
to banish
the ould flute
away;

For they
couldn't
knock heresy
out of its head,
and they bought
Bob
another
to play
in its stead.

So
the ould flute
was
doomed
and its fate
was pathetic;
it was fastened
and burned
at the stake
as a heretic.

While
the flames
roared
around it,
they heard
a strange noise –
'twas
the ould flute
still whistlin'
'The Protestant Boys'!

The Ould Orange Flute

In the County Tyrone, near the town of Dungannon,
Where many's the ruction myself had a han' in,
Bob Williamson lived, a weaver by trade,
And all of us thought him a stout Orange blade.
On the Twelfth of July, as it yearly did come,
Bob played on the flute to the sound of the drum.
You may talk of your harp, your piano, or lute,
But nothing could sound like the ould Orange flute.

But Bob the deceyver, he took us all in,
For he married a Papish called Bridget McGinn,
Turned Papish himself, and forsook the ould cause
That gave us our freedom, religion, and laws.
Now, the boys in the townland made comment upon it,
And Bob had to fly to the province of Connaught.
He flew with his wife, and his fixin's to boot,
And along with the others the ould Orange flute.

At the Chapel on Sundays to atone for past deeds,
He said 'Paters' and 'Aves' and counted his beads,
Till, after some time, at the priest's own desire,
He went with his ould flute to play in the choir.
He went with his ould flute to play in the Mass,
But the instrument shivered and sighed, Oh alas!
When he blew it and fingered and made a great noise,
The flute would play only 'The Protestant Boys'.

Bob jumped and he started and got in a splutter,
And threw the ould flute in the Bless'd Holy Water;
He thought that this charm might bring some other sound.
When he blew it again, it played 'Croppies Lie Down',
And all he could whistle and finger and blow,
To play Papish music he found it no go.
'Kick the Pope', 'The Boyne Water' and such like it would sound,
But one Papish squeak in it couldn't be found.

At a council of priests that was held the next day,
They decided to banish the ould flute away;
For they couldn't knock heresy out of its head,
And they bought Bob another to play in its stead.
So the ould flute was doomed and its fate was pathetic;
It was fastened and burned at the stake as a heretic.
While the flames roared around it, they heard a strange noise –
'Twas the ould flute still whistlin' 'The Protestant Boys'!

The Blackstaff Press
3 Galway Park, Dundonald, Belfast BT16 0AN

First published in 1983
by The Blackstaff Press
with the assistance of The Arts Council of Northern Ireland

Phototypeset in 18 on 19 pt Sabon
Printed in Northern Ireland by W & G Baird Limited

British Library Cataloguing in Publication Data

The Ould Orange flute.
1. Irish ballads and songs
I. McDonnell, Hector
821'.04 PR8780

ISBN 0-85640-290-7